© Adrian Trendall 2020
First edition 2020
ISBN: 978 1 78631 044 6

Printed in China on responsibly sourced paper on behalf of Latitude Press Ltd
A catalogue record for this book is available from the British Library.
All photographs are by the author unless otherwise stated.

Maps are reproduced with
permission from HARVEY Maps,
www.harveymaps.co.uk

Updates to this guide

While every effort is made by our authors to ensure the accuracy of guidebooks as they go to print, changes can occur during the lifetime of an edition. Any updates that we know of for this guide will be on the Cicerone website (www.cicerone.co.uk/1043/updates), so please check before planning your trip. We also advise that you check information about such things as transport, accommodation and shops locally. Even rights of way can be altered over time. We are always grateful for information about any discrepancies between a guidebook and the facts on the ground, sent by email to updates@cicerone.co.uk or by post to Cicerone, Juniper House, Murley Moss, Oxenholme Road, Kendal, Cumbria, LA9 7RL, United Kingdom.

Register your book: To sign up to receive free updates, special offers and GPX files where available, register your book at www.cicerone.co.uk.

Skye's Cuillin Ridge Traverse Topo Booklet

With Harvey 1:25,000 and 1:12,500 mapping

by Adrian Trendall

Juniper House, Murley Moss,
Oxenholme Road, Kendal, Cumbria LA9 7RL
www.cicerone.co.uk

Heading towards An Stac. The direct line takes the obvious basalt dyke but the bypass descends left and skirts up slabs (Section 5)

Contents

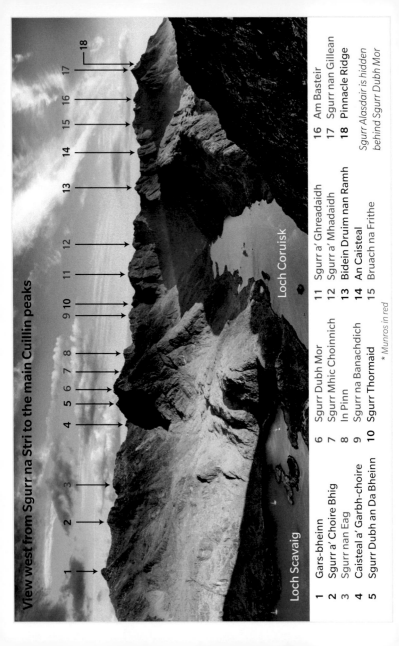

View west from Sgurr na Stri to the main Cuillin peaks

Loch Scavaig

Loch Coruisk

1 Gars-bheinn
2 Sgurr a' Choire Bhig
3 Sgurr nan Eag
4 Caisteal a' Garbh-choire
5 Sgurr Dubh an Da Bheinn

6 Sgurr Dubh Mor
7 Sgurr Mhic Choinnich
8 In Pinn
9 Sgurr na Banachdich
10 Sgurr Thormaid

11 Sgurr a' Ghreadaidh
12 Sgurr a' Mhadaidh
13 Bidein Druim nan Ramh
14 An Caisteal
15 Bruach na Frithe

16 Am Basteir
17 Sgurr nan Gillean
18 Pinnacle Ridge

Sgurr Alasdair is hidden behind Sgurr Dubh Mor

Munros in red

Route Summary Table

Section number	Section name	Time
1	Gars-bheinn to Caisteal a' Garbh-choire	1hr 30min–2hr 30min
2	Caisteal a' Garbh-choire to Thearlaich Dubh Gap	45min–1hr 30min
3	Thearlaich Dubh Gap to Sgurr Thearlaich via Sgurr Alasdair	45min
4	Sgurr Thearlaich to Bealach Coire Lagan	1hr 25min–2hr
5	Bealach Coire Lagan to Sgurr Dearg	50min–2hr
6	Sgurr Dearg to An Dorus	2hr 15min–3hr
7	An Dorus to Bealach na Glaic Moire	1hr 15min–2hr 15min
8	Bealach na Glaic Moire to Bealach Harta	1hr 30min–2hr 30min
9	Bealach Harta to Bealach nan Lice	1hr 30min–2hr 30min
10	Bealach nan Lice to Sgurr nan Gillean	1hr 30min–2hr 30min

Symbols used on maps and topos

～	route
～	alternative route
S	start point
F	finish point
>	route direction
1 **i**	numbered waymark (main route)
1 **i**	numbered waymark (alt route)
$	numbered waymark (hidden from view)
A	abseil
B	bivi site
W	water
ER→	escape route

Climber making crux moves up steep crack above pinnacle on Sgurr a' Mhadaidh's 2nd top (Section 7)

Introduction

Using this guide

The ridge has been divided into 10 sections, very much based on difficulty. Thus, Section 1 is geographically a long distance but the relatively easy nature of the terrain makes for speedy progress. Conversely, Section 8, traversing Bidein, is a short distance but over very complex terrain with hard scrambling and abseils.

The ridge is described from south to north. Each section begins with a box of summary information, which includes grade, time and terrain. Scrambling and climbing grades are used to indicate difficulty. Times are only a rough estimate since so much depends on personal fitness and experience, and prevailing conditions. Times are assumed to be for a two-day traverse carrying bivi gear by a fit, experienced team, so they may need to be adjusted. A brief description sums up the type of terrain to be expected in each section.

Each section also includes a map of the section showing start and finish points and numbered points along the route, which correlate with numbers in the accompanying text and photo topos.

The main route is marked in red with alternatives in green. Numbered waypoints (❶, ❷, ❸, etc) are sometimes subdivided further into Roman numerals (ⓘ, ⓘⓘ, ⓘⓘⓘ etc). Bivi sites abound but major ones are marked. Water sources are also marked. The ridge is escapable in many places but the more obvious escape routes are marked on the maps.

In good visibility, the map and text may suffice especially if the more complex sections have already been explored. However, it is best if map, text and photo topos are all used in conjunction. On two of the most complicated sections, there are also diagrams to clarify the route in more detail.

Any instructions, left and right, are assumed to be from facing the direction of travel (ie south to north). If there may be any confusion then additional instructions such as 'on Glen Brittle side' or on 'Loch Coruisk side' are added to clarify things.

All maps are reproduced from the Harvey Superwalker XT25 map, Skye: The Cuillin. It is recommended that you carry a hard copy of the map with you to provide an overview since each map section only covers a small area. A complete map also allows for change of plans should that be necessary. Many thanks to Harvey for agreeing to the use of their maps in this book.

Cuillin Ridge Traverse

High above Coir' a' Ghrunnda on Sgurr Dubh an Da Bheinn (Section 2)

Approaches to the ridge

There are three main approaches to Gars-bheinn, each with pros and cons. Some traversers may begin with Sgurr nan Eag, the first Munro, but this misses a classic walk and the obvious start of the ridge.

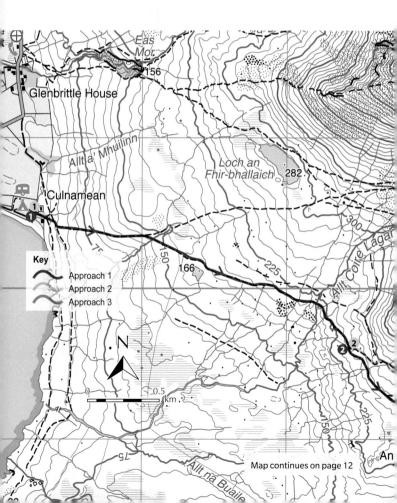

Map continues on page 12

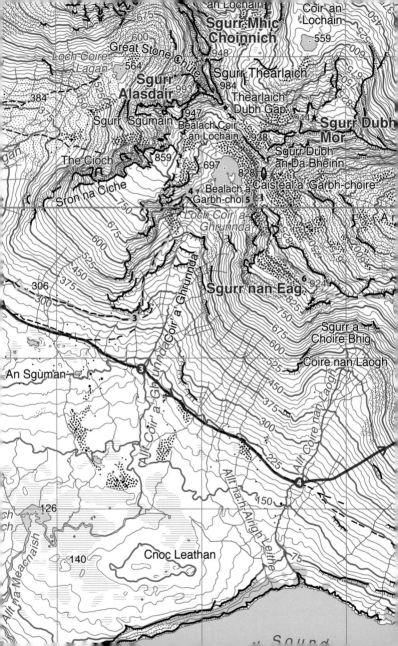

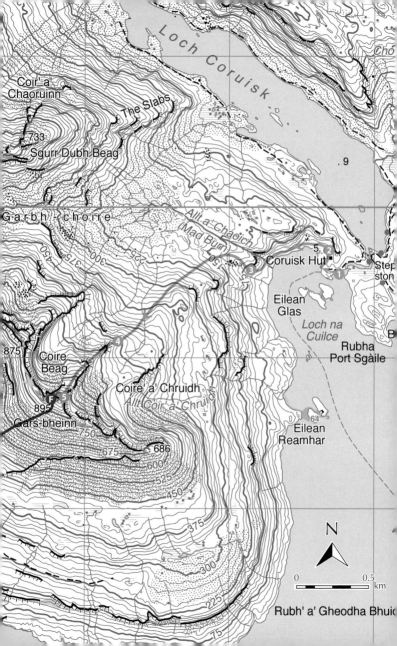

Approach 1
Glen Brittle to Gars-bheinn

Start	Glen Brittle campsite/car park.
Time	3hr.
Pros	It's a good path for much of way, fairly obvious in the dark, and fast.
Cons	It can be wet and muddy; at 6.75km, it's a longer walk than from Elgol; and it involves an interminable scree ascent of Gars-bheinn.

This is the traditional approach. Direct and popular, it's easy to follow in the dark thus good for an early start.

1 Leave Glen Brittle campsite and follow the path to Coire Lagan. Fork right and continue to below **Sron na Ciche**, reaching a path junction shortly after crossing the **Allt Coire Lagan**.

2 Take the right-hand path (this is easy to miss in dark).

3 Cross **Allt Coir' a' Ghrunnda**. The path now becomes less distinct and can be wet and muddy under foot.

4 Cross **Allt Coire nan Laogh** and ascend **Gars-bheinn's SW flank**, making sure to pick the best line up the screes. Near the top, try to keep well to the east so as to hit the ridge as close to the summit as possible.

Approach 2
Glen Brittle to Gars-bheinn via Coir' a' Ghrunnda

Start	Glen Brittle campsite/car park
Time	3hr 30min.
Pros	There's a good chance of keeping your feet dry; you can get water 100m below the ridge; the path is mostly good up to the loch.
Cons	It's a longer walk of around 7.5km; it's out and back the same way; there's extra height gain and loss.
Note	Refer to Section 1 map for this approach.

With an out-and-back repeat of the first part of the ridge, this is not the purist's choice. It's straightforward, fast and easy enough to follow in the dark and, once the ridge is gained, you can dump your packs.

1. Leave Glen Brittle campsite and follow the path to Coire Lagan. Fork right and continue to below **Sron na Ciche**, reaching a path junction shortly after crossing the **Allt Coire Lagan**.

2. Make sure you take the higher path, which continues to contour round the hillside.

3. Follow the path as it bears left and heads up towards **Coir a' Ghrunnda**.

4. Cross the outflow stream from the loch and head east.

5. After skirting the loch, zigzag up scree and rocks to the ridge and then head along it to the summit of Sgurr nan Eag.

6. From the summit of **Sgurr nan Eag**, descend then traverse **Sgurr a' Choire Bhig** to reach **Gars-bheinn**.

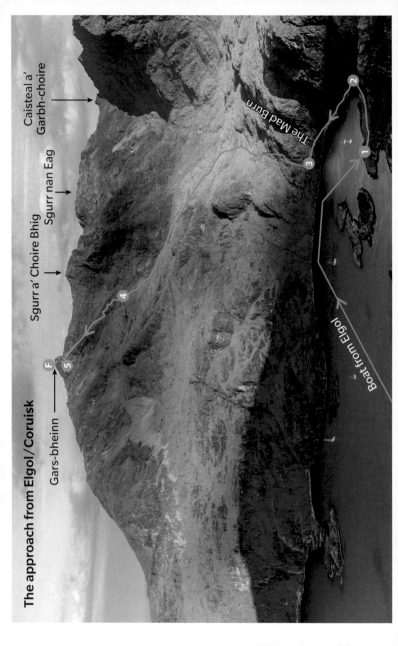

The approach from Elgol/Coruisk

Caisteal a' Garbh-choire

Sgurr nan Eag

Sgurr a' Choire Bhig

Gars-bheinn

The Mad Burn

Boat from Elgol

Approach 3
Boat from Elgol

Start	Catch the boat from Elgol.
Time	Boat trip takes 50min; allow 2hr 30min for ascent to ridge.
Pros	This approach includes a wonderful boat trip; it's usually fairly dry underfoot; you can fill water bottles high up; and it's the shortest walk-in (around 3km).
Cons	It costs £14 one way; you need to consider the logistics of retrieving your car from Elgol; and there's no chance of an alpine start.
Note	Elgol is a small fishing village with stunning views across Loch Scavaig to the Cuillin. It is approached by the B8083, a single track road from Broadford.

This the most inspiring approach with great views of the ridge, a seal colony and other wildlife. The first boat goes about 9am, with six more sailings through the day, the last being at 17:15. Alternatively, you can walk the coast path from Elgol. Many will choose to walk up to Gars-bheinn for an evening bivi before starting.

1. The boat will drop you off at the metal landing steps. Walk across grass in front of the distinctive white JMCS Hut.

2. Boulder hop along the shoreline and then cross The Mad Burn.

3. Head up before the next streambed and cross it. Begin the slog up the ridge. Fill your water bottles as high as possible.

Misty Isle about to leave Elgol with the Cuillin shrouded in cloud

4. **NE ridge, Gars-bheinn (1).** The start of the ridge proper at 600m is marked by an obvious rock nose, which can be taken direct or (more easily) bypassed to the left or right on screes. Continue up scree and rocks to the head wall above.

5. The fearsome looking headwall is outflanked by a traverse right. Descend a little to a narrow shelf below a rock band and follow it to a loose gully, which leads up to the ridge just west of the summit. Dump your packs and tick the first summit.

Ridge traverse

Section 1
Gars-bheinn to Caisteal a' Garbh-choire

Grade	1 and 2.
Time	1hr 30min–2hr 30min.
Terrain	Mostly rough hill walking with limited amounts of scrambling.
Options	These include the N ridge bypass, Sgurr nan Eag (1) (an easier option with less exposure); and the S ridge and W face of Caisteal a' Garbh-choire (Moderate).

This gentle introduction to the ridge provides stunning views of the route ahead.

Gars-bheinn ❶   **Gars-bheinn and the start of the ridge**

steep headwall

5

NE ridge approach from Coruisk

Steep scree approach from Glen Brittle

1 **W ridge, Gars-bheinn (1).** Leave the summit and scramble down to a notch in the ridge, then traverse a minor top to reach the head of a narrow gully on to the N of the crest which runs down into Coire Beag. Continue past another minor top and go along the grassy ridge passing several bivi sites.

2 **S ridge, Sgurr a' Choire Bhig (1).** Enjoy some easy scrambling up a series of short steps then walk along a narrow ridge.

3 **NW ridge, Sgurr a' Choire Bhig (walk).** Walk down the narrow ridge to reach bivi sites on slabs above the col between Sgurr a' Choire Bhig and Sgurr nan Eag.

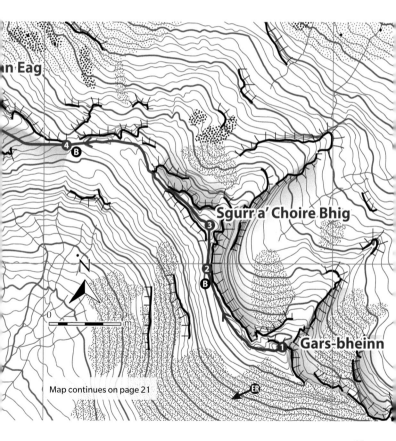

Map continues on page 21

Am Basteir

Sgurr a' Choire Bhig

Sgurr Dubh Mor

Sgurr Alasdair

Caisteal
a' Garbh-choire

Sgurr nan Eag

typical bivi site

**Leaving Gars-bheinn, having
descended from the summit**

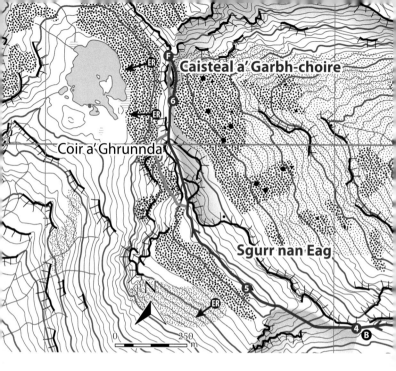

4 **SE ridge, Sgurr nan Eag (walk).** Walk up scree and rocks picking out the easiest line.

5 **N ridge, Sgurr nan Eag (2).** Take a fairly direct descent following the ridge line down to Bealach a' Gharbh-choire. Head NW from the summit then start to descend the ridge – stick closely to the crest to enjoy the best scrambling.

This section is geologically interesting, as you first descend a cone sheet, then make more complicated progress round/over large gabbro blocks then, finally, across ultra-rough peridotite down to the bealach.

N ridge bypass, Sgurr nan Eag (1). This is an easier option with less exposure. Take the less direct but easier way down to the left of the crest, which is mostly on scree with only some minor scrambling. Finally, pick your way through a jumble of large peridotite blocks to reach Bealach a' Garbh-choire

---

6 **Caisteal a' Garbh-choire bypass (walk).** Most people bypass this imposing block of peridotite to save time by weaving between large blocks to the east (Coruisk side). The section ends immediately north of Caisteal a' Garbh-choire. An interesting cave under a boulder leads down to Coir' a' Ghrunnda while to the north is the N ridge of Sgurr Dubh an Da Bheinn.

S ridge and W face, Caisteal a' Garbh-choire (Moderate). This is at the top end of the grade but the rough rock offsets the exposure and steepness. It's a highly recommended option for teams that are going well and relish an extra challenge.

Scramble up from the bealach until the crest steepens then climb up slightly left of the crest in an exposed position. The final moves are awkward but can be well protected.

Continue along the crest and either descend the middle of the W face and scramble around to the NW side and scramble up loose ground to emerge by a tunnel under a massive leaning block or descend left from the ridge towards Coir' a' Ghrunnda then contour round to the right to reach the northern end. Alternatively, make a very steep 13m abseil from a very low boulder usually with in situ slings.

Morning light on scramblers doing the ridge in a day

Section 2

Caisteal a' Garbh-choire to the Thearlaich Dubh Gap

Grade	Grade 2 scrambling, an Easy/Moderate climb and an abseil.
Time	45min–1hr 30min. Will depend largely on whether or not Sgurr Dubh Mor is visited.
Terrain	Lots of scrambling, walking and an easy climb.

The interest increases as the terrain becomes more rugged with grade 2 scrambling, a climb, an abseil and the option to tick an extra Munro.

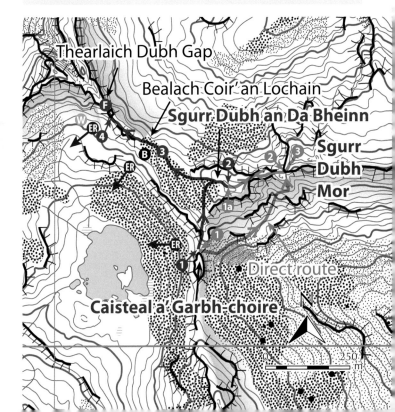

❶ **S ridge, Sgurr Dubh an Da Bheinn (2).** Section 2 starts with some lovely scrambling on extremely rough rock with much variation possible. Head N from **Caisteal a' Garbh-choire** and scramble up blocks generally just left of the crest on the Coir' a' Ghrunnda side.

Continue up until the angle eases off and then trend right to the summit.

Sgurr Dubh Mor option. Historically not included as part of the traverse, lots of people visit this outlying peak and seize the opportunity to tick another Munro. You should only consider doing this if you moving swiftly, are on schedule and visibility is good. Unless you are speeding, allow an hour for the out-and-back journey.

If you are doing Sgurr Dubh Mor, it's worth considering the direct route **❶** out to it from Caisteal a' Garbh-choire. This route has a lot of very loose rocks and is only recommended in good visibility or if you know the route. In poor visibility, use the E ridge of Sgurr Dubh an Da Bheinn **❶a**.

❶ **Direct route.** From Caisteal a' Garbh-choire, contour round to the NE above An Garbh-choire to reach a slabby wall, which allows access to a rubble filled gully. This leads up to join the route out to Sgurr Dubh Mor from Sgurr Dubh an Da Bheinn.

❶a **E ridge, Sgurr Dubh an Da Bheinn (1).** Leave the summit, pass a bivi site and scramble fairly easily down the ridge to a low point at 886m. Large pinnacles can be taken direct but are much more easily bypassed to the right (S).

❷ **SW spur, Sgurr Dubh Mor (2).** This part is fairly complex with lots of paths and signs of wear. Much of it involves walking but even the easiest way requires scrambling (and it all has to be reversed for the return trip). In general, the easiest lines are to the right (S).

    ⅰ Pass distinct brown rocks and continue on path that contours round before scrambling up short, rock steps. Ascend a gully by slabs and loose rocks. At the top, turn right along a path ledge.

    ⅱ Ignore the continuing ledge/path and turn left, climbing a groove to reach another traverse line.

    ⅲ Turn right and continue until below an obvious jutting out block. Climb up to the block, go through a gap and traverse back left and then cut back right to reach the summit plateau.

❸ Summit **Sgurr Dubh Mor** before returning to Sgurr Dubh an Da Bheinn.

SW spur, Sgurr Dubh Mor

gap

← jutting rock

traverse path/ledge

slab

traverse path/ledge

gully

Sgurr Dubh an Da Bheinn

2 **NW ridge, Sgurr Dubh an Da Bheinn (1).** Continue walking; scramble down a few short steps.

The approach to T-D Gap
seen from Sgurr Dubh
an Da Bheinn

Sgurr
Alasdair

Sgurr
Thearlaich

A

F

4

Outline of buttress
before T-D Gap

Bealach Coir' an Lochain

3

Approach to and abseil into the T-D Gap

T-D Gap

A

F

4

Bealach Coir' an Lochain

3

3 **Bealach Coir' an Lochain (walk).** Stay switched on across this easy terrain, as it's easy to become disorientated, especially in poor visibility.

4 **Approach to the T-D Gap (Easy/Moderate).** The ridge narrows before the T-D Gap and rears up into a tower. Move left onto a steep wall and climb it in a very exposed position. This climb is serious, exposed and on some loose rock so, if in doubt, rope up.

Once the angle eases off, head up and right to an abseil point with in situ slings on the edge of the T-D Gap. This offers a good viewpoint to check out the climb in the wall opposite.

Abseil (10m) down a steep wall to the highest point of the gully, which forms the **T-D Gap**.

Approach to the T-D Gap

4

Section 3
Thearlaich Dubh Gap to Sgurr Thearlaich via Sgurr Alasdair

Grade	Severe with a grade 3 alternative.
Time	45min is reasonably fast but it largely depends on your climbing ability, the conditions and whether you need to carry or haul packs or queue at the T-D Gap.
Terrain	Hard climbing to exit the Gap and lots of scrambling.

Technicalities ramp up in this section with, arguably, the hardest pitch on the ridge. While Sgurr Alasdair is not directly on the ridge, it is a Munro, the highest peak on Skye and only a short excursion, so virtually everyone visits it.

A quality bypass is included, should time, conditions or psyche be against you.

❶ **T-D Gap Original Route (Severe, 20m).** The T-D Gap has a reputation. The climb is polished and treacherous if wet. It is best described as 'traditional' so be prepared for a struggle especially with a large pack. It is possible to haul packs but the nature of the rock makes jamming a possibility. You'll find 120cm or even 240cm slings useful for threads.

Belay below the obvious corner/crack opposite the abseil using a high thread.

❶ The steep climbing is well protected with a thread.

❷ A sling over a spike and/or a rock placement provides further protection.

❸ A rock 3 placement hidden (behind the climber) protects the crux moves to reach the horizontal ledge out to the left at 8m. Make sure the rock 3 is well extended to reduce the chance of it lifting out as you climb past. Face leftwards and squirm up to grasp the sharp-edged ledge.

❹ Mantle up onto the ledge and the route is in the bag but take care not to run things out too much. Too often climbers with big packs do the crux then run it out to the top with no gear placed.

❺ Things ease off now and you'll reach a small cave at 16m (good thread). Step left above the cave.

❻ Reach a belay above. There are usually slings in situ on a block.

The T-D Gap (Severe, 20m)
Facing left, making the crux moves to
reach horizontal ledge up and to the left

sharp edged ledge

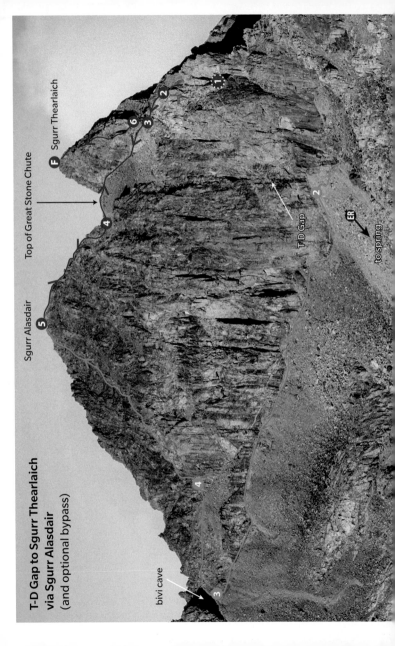

T-D Gap to Sgurr Thearlaich
via Sgurr Alasdair
(and optional bypass)

Sgurr Alasdair

Top of Great Stone Chute

bivi cave

Sgurr Thearlaich

T-D Gap

ER

to spring

2 SE ridge, Sgurr Thearlaich (2). Enjoy pleasant scrambling above the T-D Gap.

3 Around 30m above T-D Gap, follow an easy traverse left along distinct strata and onto a scree slope, which leads to the top of the Great Stone Chute.

4 SE ridge, Sgurr Alasdair (2). From the top of the **Great Stone Chute** (955m), follow the crest to the summit. The way is well worn and ascends short steps and slabs. It is exposed with spectacular views to the Stone Chute below and the ridge ahead.

5 From the summit, retrace your route to the Stone Chute and back onto Sgurr Thearlaich's SE ridge. It is possible to avoid the descent and retracing your steps back towards the TD-Gap by a more direct entry onto the SE ridge. This is harder but only for a couple of moves.

T-D Gap bypass (walk and 3). This is a useful alternative if the T-D Gap is busy or the rock is wet.

1 You can either decide to miss the Gap entirely and continue from Bealach Coir' an Lochain along the ridge then descend after a small rise and descend to the entrance of the T-D Gap.

Or, having abseiled into the T-D Gap and decided to give it a miss, descend T-D Gap Gully (grade 2, 65m). It's mostly fairly easy but loose with a steeper and harder step at the base. There are often threaded abseil slings in situ under the jammed boulders at the top of the gully.

2 Traverse screes below the cliff along a worn path immediately below the cliffs and ascend scree to a good **bivi cave** just below Bealach Sgumain with its distinctive pinnacles silhouetted on the skyline.

3 Ascend to the right of the cave and head for a left-facing chimney/corner about 50m to the east of the bealach and 20m lower.

4 SW flank, Sgurr Alasdair (3). Scramble up the polished 25m chimney and climb the left wall (crux) before making an exit to the right. Either zigzag up the shallow scoop above and follow it to the summit of Sgurr Alasdair, or, better still, cut back left to the narrow SW ridge, which you follow in fine positions to the summit.

T-D Gap bypass

Sgurr Dubh an Da Bheinn

Sgurr Dubh Mor

T-D Gap

T-D Gap

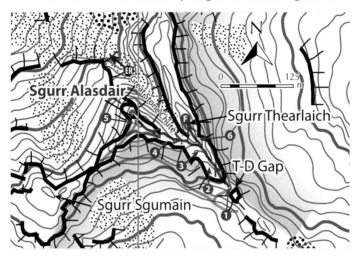

❻ **S ridge, Sgurr Thearlaich (3)**. This connects the SE ridge to the summit. Having regained the ridge crest via the distinct strata, carry on up towards the summit.

When the ridge narrows, move on to its right (E) side. Some enjoyable grade 3 scrambling will lead you to the summit of Sgurr Thearlaich.

Section 4

Sgurr Thearlaich to Bealach Coire Lagan

Grade	Sustained scrambling and climbing to Very Difficult (optional Collie's Ledge reduces grade to Moderate).
Time	1hr 25min–2hr.
Terrain	It's very exposed with lots of slabs, which can be treacherous if wet. The upper slabs of Sgurr Mhic Choinnich are basalt and notoriously slippery if wet.

This is complex terrain that should not be underestimated. There is a variant descent from the summit of Sgurr Thearlaich to Bealach Mhic Choinnich. It is possible to stick to the ridge or take a Western Bypass but there are good reasons that local guides opt for the Eastern Traverse as, once the start is located, it is the quickest and easiest route.

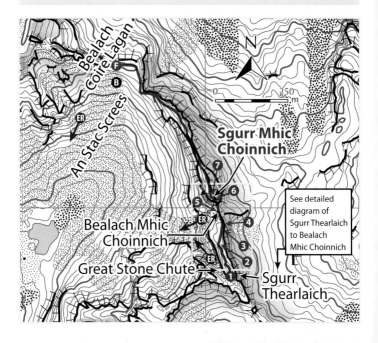

The descent from Sgurr Thearlaich

7 Sgurr Mhic Choinnich

Collie's Ledge

King's Chimney

6

5

Second gap

2

4

3

First gap in
the ridge

Sgurr Alasdair

Sgurr Thearlaich **1**

~ Eastern Traverse
~ Western Bypass

First gap

Second gap

Great Stone Chute

2

bivi

i

3

4

ii

slab

boulder

iii

iv

pillar

Bealach Mhic
Choinnich

5

**Descent from Sgurr Thearlaich
to Bealach Mhic Choinnich**

❶ **N ridge, Sgurr Thearlaich (Moderate).** Descend roof-like slabs from the summit of Sgurr Thearlaich. Cross one gap in the crest and continue along to a second gap.

❷ Just beyond the second gap, (about 100m before the steep nose above Bealach Mhic Choinnich), descend to the right (E) following slight signs of a path/general wear and tear. Go round a corner to the left and along ledges to the crux.

❸ Down-climb the 10m wall, which is awkward but only Moderate if dry. Slings are occasionally in situ where people have abseiled. This is very exposed with big drops below so, if in doubt, use a rope.

❹ Follow ledges below to another, easier and shorter down-climb. This leads to another ledge below, which leads around and down to Bealach Mhic Choinnich. The descent is exposed and sometimes there is a threaded sling in situ.

Western Bypass (Moderate). From the second gap, carry on to where the ridge flattens out and there is a distinctive stone-walled bivi site.

ⓘ Go down a small NW facing slot with knee-high rocks either side. This slot is down and left of the bivi site. Descend a steep rib for 5m. This is very exposed (Moderate) and descends a dyke.

ⓘⓘ From the base of the rib, cut back right below a steep wall. Traverse slabs as high as possible, pass behind a boulder and carry on to the halfway ledge.

ⓘⓘⓘ Descend loose rock diagonally left down a gully to a small pillar.

ⓘⓥ Descend a chimney to the right of the pillar. Traverse right across unusual, rubbly rock and go up to Bealach Mhic Choinnich.

---

❺ From Bealach Mhic Choinnich, you have a choice of a classic climb or an exposed walk/scramble. King's Chimney and Collie's Ledge both have the same start to exit the bealach. From **Bealach Mhic Choinnich**, move 6m right (E) to a slab and short corner. Climb steeply but on good holds to gain the obvious traverse line of Collie's Ledge, which leads back left.

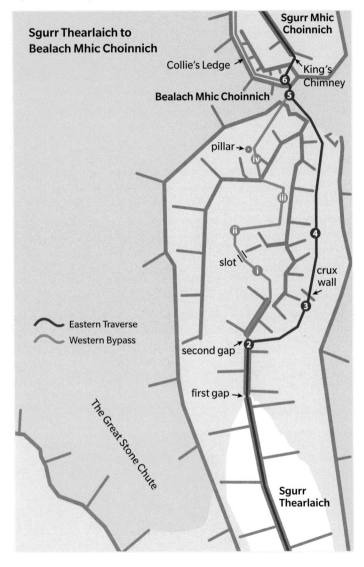

6 **King's Chimney, Sgurr Mhic Choinnich (Very Difficult, 25m).** More corner than chimney, this is a classic that should not be missed if conditions and time allow. It's also easier than it looks – as long as it's dry. Rock 6 and Rockcentric 3 are useful, as are 120cm slings for the chockstones.

Scramble up the obvious, steep ramp going right from the start of the traverse of Collie's Ledge to:

i Belay on a ledge below the corner.

ii Climb the wide corner/crack on good gabbro passing chockstones (good threads).

iii Traverse out right on good but well-spaced holds to outflank the overhang.

iv Finish more easily.

v Arrive at a block belay with a good view down the route.

Follow the exposed crest north for about 55m to the summit.

King's Chimney

Traverse of Sgurr Mhic Choinnich

Sgurr Mhic Choinnich

7

King's Chimney

6

Collie's Ledge

Bealach Mhic Choinnich

Great Stone Chute

Rotten Gully

Bealach Coire Lagan

F

Collie's Ledge

Collie's Ledge (Moderate) option. This route enables you to enjoy sensational positions as you traverse high above Coire Lagan. A relatively easy route across improbable looking terrain, it's a good alternative to King's Chimney and fast since you, hopefully, won't need a rope.

After the initial boulder problem start it's basically a walk with Grade 2 scrambling.

Continue under King's Chimney along a rising traverse line to reach an exposed nose where the route crosses the west buttress.

After turning a corner, go down to a scree path interspersed with a couple of short scrambles. Cross another nose of rock then delicately traverse a steep rock band and continue easily to a distinctive chimney, which marks the junction with the N ridge.

Follow N ridge to the summit.

7 **N Ridge, Sgurr Mhic Choinnich (3)**. This is a narrow, beautifully situated ridge but the upper basalt section is slippery if wet. Descend 200m to just below a small rise where Collie's Ledge enters from the left. Continue down the fairly easy terrain then scramble over blocks and down grooves. Make sure to descend far enough to outflank the in cut of **Rotten Gully** then ascend to a plateau and cross to **Bealach Coire Lagan**.

Climber on An Stac Direct with Bealach Coire Lagan and the An Stac screes visible below

Section 5

Bealach Coire Lagan to Sgurr Dearg

Grade	Climbing to Moderate and extensive grade 3 scrambling if An Stac is taken direct.
Time	50min–2hr, but timing is very dependent on how busy the Inaccessible Pinnacle (In Pinn) is when you arrive.
Terrain	Very exposed scrambling and climbing.

This section gives you the choice of a classic scramble or an easier and quicker bypass to arrive at the iconic In Pinn.

❶ An Stac direct (3, 250m). This involves some impressive scrambling up the longest single vertical section of the whole ridge. It is a serious undertaking and inescapable, although its reputation for loose rock has been exaggerated. Not to be underestimated, increasingly steep and exposed, this should only be attempted by confident scramblers.

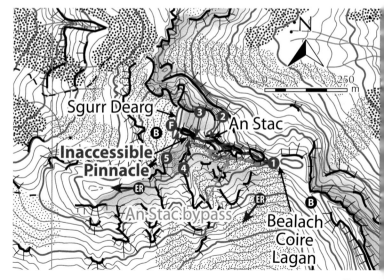

An Stac direct and the An Stac bypass

The In Pinn

A **4**

F

5

An Stac

2

3

vi

v

An Stac Chimney

small notch

iv

U-shaped notch

An Stac bypass

iii

Bealach Coire Lagan

ii

i

ⅰ Ascend an obvious ramp 10m left (S) of the crest and just beyond a notch at the NW end of the bealach. This dyke is typical of much of the route.

ⅱ Cross easy terrain to an obvious **U-shaped notch** in the ridge to your right.

ⅲ Scree slopes left of the notch offer a last chance to escape – otherwise, the only way is up. Climb a dyke/chimney just left of the crest to another, smaller notch.

ⅳ The crest above is narrows and steepens. Traverse left to access the crest, which is followed for about 80m to where An Stac Chimney joins from the left. It's very exposed but on good holds.

ⅴ Follow the obvious chimney to its top.

ⅵ Above the chimney, the terrain levels off. Traverse left then up easy corners to the summit of An Stac.

❷ Descend easily and pass a stone bivi circle to reach the base of the In Pinn (3).

An Stac bypass (2). This is a much easier alternative and especially useful if time or weather dictates avoiding the direct route. It follows an orange coloured ramp and screes and, being faster, does provide the chance to overtake parties before the bottleneck of the In Pinn.

From Bealach Coire Lagan, descend rock steps and scree to an obvious path going up screes below the bulk of An Stac. Carry on in the same line up slabs, rocks and screes. Pass through a gap by some large boulders, veer right and then scramble up to a higher ramp line and continue up to the base of the In Pinn.

---

❸ E ridge, In Pinn (Moderate, 65m). The In Pinn is potentially the biggest bottleneck on the ridge, with lots of guided groups and individuals a distinct possibility if the conditions are good. Be prepared for queues or, better still, try and time your arrival to be outside peak hours of mid morning to mid afternoon. On a two-day traverse, it's possible you will arrive late on the first day and find the crag empty. Teams doing the ridge in a day will be under more time pressure but are, hopefully, experienced enough to solo or move fast enough to overtake others.

Traditional etiquette is that priority should be given to those doing the ridge in a day (ie moving quite fast and solo or using minimal gear, perhaps moving together). Be polite and see if other people will let you past but be aware of the risks, especially if soloing. If you are forced to queue, then use the time productively; eat and drink, and look at the route ahead on the map.

The E ridge of the In Pinn

4

abseil point →

NB there are at least 15 people
visible, a clue to how busy it
can get at times

F

ii usual
belay

5 **i** possible
belay

3

An Stac bypass

Route from An Stac direct

Start near the eastern end of the south face (around 8m from lowest part of the E ridge). Climb a broken chimney and go up along a ramp parallel to the E ridge to a possible belay.

i Leave the **possible belay** and gain the ridge and just above is the crux of the climb where the ridge briefly steepens. A very exposed couple of moves can be protected by a sling on a small spike. Better holds will soon appear and you'll reach the more **usual belay** at 30m. This is a ledge on the Coruisk side with large spike and block belays.

ii Above the belay, things are easier and the ridge widens out. Belay on blocks overlooking a ledge that leads around the Bolster Stone (technically the highest point)

The E ridge probably takes 99% of the traffic and is often jammed so an alternative is **S crack (Hard Very Difficult, 30m)**. Another classic climb, it is harder but well protected. It takes the obvious crack in the middle of the S face. It bypasses much of the E ridge so missing the queues and providing an overtaking lane if you're fast (not shown on topo).

4 **Descent of In Pinn.** From the summit, follow the ledge right of the Bolster Stone to in situ maillons. The usual descent is to abseil the W ridge. Skilled climbers may down-climb (severe). A 35m rope doubled will reach the ground. Most hold-ups occur with people queuing to abseil so try and think outside the box. Use other anchors and get other people to throw your sling down or share ropes with other parties.

5 Head up the slabs to the ridge that overlooks the In Pinn. **Sgurr Dearg** is 978m, only 8m lower than the In Pinn.

Panorama from Sgurr na Banachdich. Loch Coruisk below and distinctive shape of Sgurr Thormaid then the 3 teeth and Sgurr a Ghreadaidh on the left

Section 6

Sgurr Dearg to An Dorus

Grade	Grade 3 with a few Moderate moves down to An Dorus.
Time	2hr 15min–3hr.
Terrain	Walking and sustained scrambling.

This section gives you the chance to cover a lot of ground relatively quickly before the magnificent S ridge of Sgurr a' Ghreadaidh and descent to An Dorus, the notional midpoint of the ridge.

❶ **NW flank, Sgurr Dearg (1).** This is a tedious descent on loose scree but has the bonus of being fast and straightforward. Do not be tempted to head N – it appears more direct but steep cliffs block the way.

Directly above the In Pinn, a small gap in Sgurr Dearg's summit ridge signals the start of the descent. Head more W than N and descend to a narrowing of the ridge at 900m then turn right to head N and descend slabs to **Bealach Coire na Banachdich**, which is very narrow, being only a few metres wide.

Note: Down to the W is the top of an obvious gorge and water can be found just above this. You may require a cup/straw to access it between boulders. Bivi sites can be found SE from the head of the gorge.

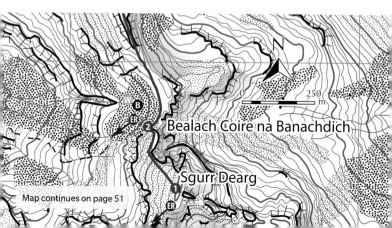

Map continues on page 51

Sgurr na
Banachdich
965m

3

942m

Sgurr Thormaid

917m

Three Teeth

Sgurr a' Ghreadaidh

878m

2 Bealach Coire na Banachdich

Bealach na Banachdich to Sgurr na Banachdich

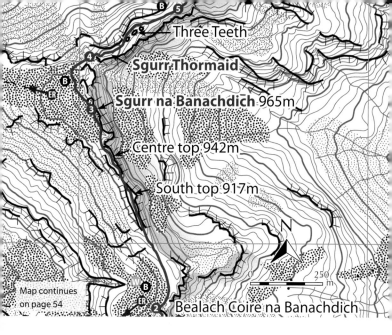

2 S ridge, Sgurr na Banachdich (2). Enjoy some easy scrambling and walking with spectacular drops off to the right. Exit the bealach to the W and contour round on scree/path to bypass point 878m and reach the start of the S ridge.

Ledges/paths on the Coire na Banachdich (W) side of the ridge provide the easiest line but you should stick to the ridge to enjoy spectacular views and scrambling. Lovely scrambling will take you over the very narrow S top (917m).

Continue over the 942m centre top, and descend steeply via a shallow gully to the W to reach an obvious dip before the main summit. Scramble up rocks then (more easily) up a cone sheet and continue to the summit to a small cairn.

3 N ridge, Sgurr na Banachdich (1/2). Descend slightly NW to avoid steep cliffs before descending N then E to the bealach before Sgurr Thormaid. Do not descend too soon or you will find your way blocked by huge cliffs.

4 From Bealach Thormaid, the ridge takes a sharp turn right. Pass left of pinnacles before heading directly up steeper rocks on the crest above the bealach. Follow the easier ground to the summit of **Sgurr Thormaid** (926m).

Descend slabs slightly right of the crest to reach the **Three Teeth**, a group of distinctive pinnacles. These are usually bypassed on the Coruisk side by a faint path but can be climbed direct at Very Difficult or bypassed on the Glen Brittle

Sgurr na Banachdich to An Dorus

Main top 973m **6**
South top 969m **ii**

i

5

S ridge, Sgurr a' Ghreadaidh

side. Regain the crest and follow it to a broad dip just before the start of the S ridge of Sgurr a' Ghreadaidh.

5 **S ridge, Sgurr a Ghreadaidh (3).** This is classic Cuillin climbing up a fantastic ridge that is quite committing but not overly technical. The hardest scrambling is between the two tops. Generally, difficulties are turned to the left on easier but looser terrain but stay on the actual crest as far as possible for the best experience.

i Leave the col and follow the ridge, which becomes narrower and more exposed as height is gained and the S summit is reached. Alternatively, take easier paths/ledges down left from the crest on the Glen Brittle side.

ii From the S summit, contemplate the difficulties barring access to the main summit; a knife-edge ridge between the two summits is unavoidable.

The crux succumbs to a variety of techniques; it can be negotiated astride or à la tightrope walker, depending on your bravery and ability, and the conditions. There is lots of exposure, especially the moves on the Coruisk side. Climb down an exposed *arête* (sharp ridge) to a dip then climb out more easily to a steep nose, which can be taken direct or bypassed by a path/ledge to the left. Continue more easily to the main summit at 973m.

6 **NE ridge, Sgurr a Ghreadaidh (3).** This is easy scrambling, apart from the down-climb to An Dorus, which has a couple of Moderate moves. Head N from the summit then descend on the left, Glen Brittle side.

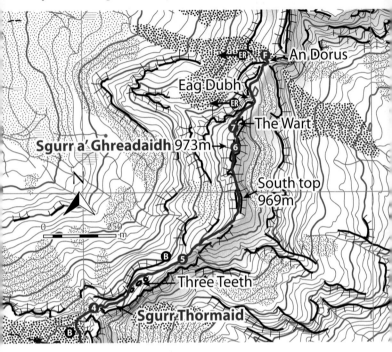

7 Continue down on the left to bypass the steep cliff known as **The Wart**. Carry on down slabs, then climb down an awkward overlap to the deep cut gully of **Eag Dubh** coming in from the left. Bypass the mouth of the gully towards the Coruisk side.

Turn left up slabs and continue down the ridge until the steep sided notch of An Dorus prevents any further progress. Down-climb a steep 3m wall in an exposed position. This involves a couple of hard moves down a corner/ramp towards the Glen Brittle side of the gap.

Congratulations are in order since **An Dorus** is normally taken to be the mid-point of a traverse but, personally, it always feels more than half-way.

Section 7

An Dorus to Bealach na Glaic Moire

Grade	Short climbs to Difficult, and lots of scrambling.
Time	1hr 15min–2hr 15min.
Terrain	Exposed climbing and scrambling.

A committing section with sustained scrambling, some short climbs and complex route finding, this is the hardest and most complex section of the whole ridge not to have a bypass.

❶ SW ridge, Sgurr a' Mhadaidh (2/3). This is a fairly obvious ascent and much used by Munro baggers. The crux is the 5m exit climb out of An Dorus followed by pleasant ridge scrambling with airy moves just below the summit. Either climb out of the gap on good holds opposite the descent, or climb the easier grooves to the right.

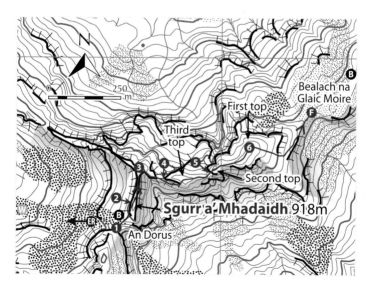

An Dorus to Bealach na Glaic Moire

2 918m

3

third top

second top

first top

6

F

Bealach na Glaic Moire

5

4

1 An Dorus

Descent to Sgurr a' Mhadaidh's third top

Pass bivi sites then turn the crest by scree/paths on the Glen Brittle side until you're forced back onto the actual crest, which leads to the summit. Traverse a slab on the Coruisk side using a horizontal crack to gain the summit.

2 Descend the Alpinesque ridge until the **Sgurr Thuilm** spur joins the main ridge from the Glen Brittle side.

3 The way ahead is blocked by a broad tower. The main ridge turns sharply turn to the right (E). Just before the **tower**, leave the roof-like crest and descend slabs on the right (Coruisk) side. If conditions are dry then the easiest and quickest way is to continue down the slab until the way is blocked by the top of **Deep Gash Gully**. This is a smooth slab with big drops below and not a place to be if the rock is wet.

Scramble down into the gully and exit by climbing the short wall opposite. Descend a narrow, slabby ridge to a levelling off below the third top.

An alternative is to climb the tower, which is steep but the holds are good. Descend to the right and join slabs leading down to the third top.

57

View of route over Sgurr a' Mhadaidh's third, second and first tops

4 Third top (Moderate). Follow signs of a path below and right of the third top. This descends slightly on the Coruisk side. Descend about 30m then zigzag up left to the S face of the third top. From the top of the path/worn ground, work your way up a series of slabs/corners to the summit.

This is a personal preference. The slabs/corners have some lovely moves and rock but like all routes here, are loose higher up. Also popular is a series of corners to the left of the suggested route. These are just right of the prow of the third top and you walk under them for the suggested route. Also Moderate, the line follows two corners to reach easier ground. Descend to the foot of the second top.

First top
6
Second top
Third top
5
steep slabs and corners
grassy ledges
zigzag up grass and rock
ignore path continuing down
Third top of Mhadaidh
4

Climbers on second top of
Sgurr a' Mhadaidh
(Difficult)

Climber on looser ground above slabs/corners leading up to Sgurr a' Mhadaidh's 3rd top

⑤ Second top (Difficult). A steep tower above guards the second top and is the crux of this section of the traverse. It looks harder than it actually is and although it has great exposure, the holds and protection (if needed) are very good.

Climb boulders then traverse out leftwards to reach a shallow corner, which trends back rightwards. The shallow corner leads to a flake/pedestal split by a steep crack. Steep moves on good holds lead to the top of the pedestal.

Above the pedestal, steep, exposed moves on good holds lead to the top (a few Difficult moves). This steep crack is exposed but easily protected and the holds are good. At the top, a good block makes for a secure belay. Continue easily to the summit.

An easy descent leads to a deep cut gully where the ridge is bisected by a thin dyke. Turn right then cut back left down to the base of the gully. Climb the steep wall on the opposite side. Continue easily to the summit of the **first top**.

⑥ Descend scree slopes on the Coruisk side and contour round to **Bealach na Glaic Moire**.

Section 8

Bealach na Glaic Moire to Bealach Harta

Grade	Lots of grade 3 and some Moderate climbing (or a bypass walk).
Time	1hr 30min–2hr 30min.
Terrain	Sustained scrambling/climbing and abseils. If time or weather dictate, there is a quick, easy bypass.

This is a very complicated section with awkward route-finding and many people waste a lot of time here.

1 Leave the bealach and head up and left towards the west ridge of the West top.

2 W ridge of West top (1). This mainly involves walking but also scrambling up basalt dyke staircases. Ascend an initial basalt dyke staircase then the ridge

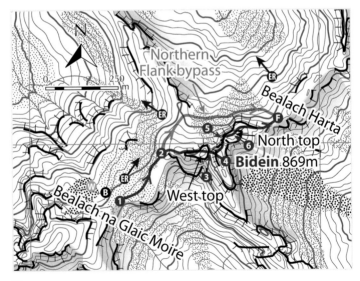

above, which leads to a second dyke staircase. This dyke is a distinctive orange colour and has an overhanging block at the top so mind your head. The house-sized summit block is bypassed on the right.

The Northern Flank bypass (walk, 30min). A fast alternative if time/conditions are against you, this has the potential to save you an hour or so but misses a classic mountain.

Go NE from the bealach along the broad ridge until the terrain steepens and you turn left and meet the ridge coming in from Sgurr an Fheadain to the NW.

Descend this ridge to just above the narrow neck at 750m then contour around on screes to a low point of 720m. Continue round close to the steep cliffs of the north top before ascending scree to Bealach Harta.

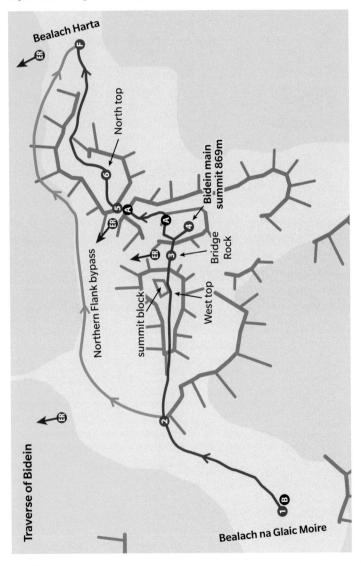

Bealach Harta

F

ER

North top

6

Bidein main
summit 869m

5 A

ER

A

4

3 ER

Bridge
Rock

Northern Flank bypass

West top

summit block

Traverse of Bidein

ER

2

ER

1 B

Bealach na Glaic Moire

E flank (Moderate). Descend slabs on the Coruisk side of the summit block. The last few moves are awkward especially with a large pack. It's very exposed with drops into the gully below. Often, you'll find an in situ sling where people have abseiled. Continue to reach the **Bridge Rock** in the gully below, which separates the West top from the main summit.

E flank of West top descent to Bridge Rock

West top summit block

rock that often has an abseil sling on

Bridge Rock

3

Bridge Rock to Bidein
main summit (lower part)

basalt dyke

easier alternative

good belay block

easier alternative

Bridge Rock

❸ W flank, main summit (3). From the Bridge Rock in the gully, climb straight up corners above then traverse left on easier ground.

> An **easier alternative** involves climbing up a few metres from the Bridge Rock before traversing right along a narrow ledge. Cut back left to join the main route.

Ascend an obvious dyke/chimney (crux) and at its top take a horizontal ledge right and continue up to a dip before the summit, which is up and right.

to summit

to abseil

basalt dyke

easier alternative

good belay block

Bridge Rock to Bidein main summit (upper part) and route to abseil

Bidein main summit **4**

Descent from Bidein main summit

i → abseil slings

small peak

ii → abseil slings

sharp edge

5

❹ NE ridge, main summit (Difficult or abseil). This descent is the most complicated and least obvious of the whole ridge. It can be down-climbed at Difficult but most people choose to abseil from the in situ slings. From the summit, there is no obvious descent. Step back down to the dip then either follow the roof-like crest of the ridge N before descending to a crevassed block with a small stance and slings; or from the dip below the summit, retrace your steps to the horizontal ledge and follow it parallel to the ridge above then descend slabs to the abseil point.

ⓘ Abseil to the base of the slabs.

> Or, down-climb the slabs (Difficult).

Leave the narrow gap at the base of the abseil/slabs and pass to the left of a **small peak**. Continue descending towards the North top until the way ahead is blocked by a steep sided gully.

ⓘ Abseil about 10m from **in situ** slings. The wall is steeply undercut with a sharp edge that your rope has to run over so be careful to avoid a swing.

> Or down-climb slabs. Descend a series of overhanging steps SE of the abseil. This is at least Difficult and harder for short people.

❺ W face, North top (3). This section looks very intimidating but is actually fairly straightforward scrambling. From the base of the abseil, traverse up and left. Follow a distinctive intrusion line curving leftwards then turn right and follow the ridge towards the summit. The rock steepens and you will reach the summit via exposed climbing on good holds in a brilliant position.

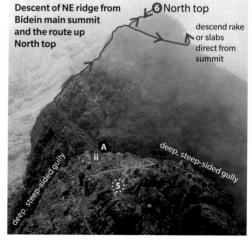

Descent of NE ridge from **Bidein main summit and the route up North top**

❻ North top

descend rake or slabs direct from summit

deep, steep-sided gully

deep, steep-sided gully

6 NE ridge of North top (2). The descent to **Bealach Harta** is open to much variation, by following a loose rake on the Coruisk side or, better still, by descending
slabs just right of the ridge.

Descent North top, Bidein,
to Bealach Harta

Bidein
main summit, 869m
4

6 North top,
852m

abseil

Bealach Harta **F**

Section 9

Bealach Harta to Bealach nan Lice

Grade	Mostly grade 2, plus an abseil (can be down-climbed at Moderate).
Time	1hr 30min–2hr 30min.
Terrain	Easy scrambling, an abseil and lots of walking and ascent.

This is a straightforward section of the ridge, but it can seem a long, hard slog to the summit of Bruach na Frithe.

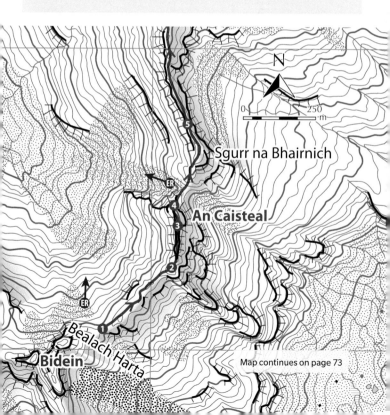

Map continues on page 73

Bealach Harta to the start of
Bruach na Frithe's S ridge

Bealach Harta **1**

2

Sgurr nan Gillean

An Caisteal summit **3**

distinctive col and
orange scree

4 abseil

Sgurr na Bairnich

Am Basteir

5

❶ Leave Bealach Harta and turn the steep nose which blocks the way by ledges slanting up to the right. The nose can be taken direct by a steep groove at grade 3.

❷ S ridge, An Caisteal (2). Follow the crest, which is cut by three gaps. The first two are bypassed by ledges on the left, the third can be jumped by the confident (more cautious people will descend a slab to the right or east to the base of the gap). Continue to the summit where there is a small cairn.

Do not proceed beyond the summit or you will end up at the infamous "Belly Crawl" abseil point. Retrace your steps south to orange rocks.

❸ N ridge, An Caisteal (3 and abseil or Moderate down-climb). At the orange rocks, turn sharply NW and cross the ridge to the Glen Brittle side. Descend fairly steeply and contour round to a levelling off. This distinctive orange/brown col is above a very obvious orange slab. Follow a groove/gully down the slab before turning left to either descend the narrow and exposed N ridge to a deep gully, which bars further progress, or traverse below the crest on the Harta Corrie side which involves down-climbing a short wall (2).

❹ Most people abseil from the slings but the down-climb is nowhere near as hard as it looks and the crux (Moderate) is right at the end just above the ground. Climb

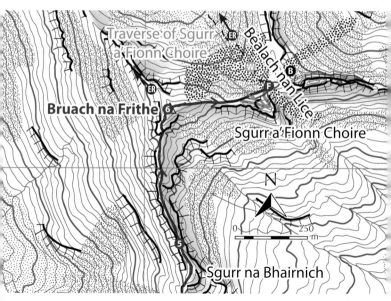

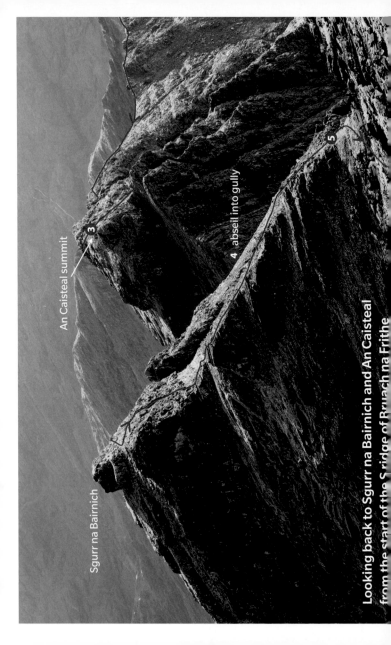

Sgurr na Bairnich

An Caisteal summit

3

4 abseil into gully

5

Looking back to Sgurr na Bairnich and An Caisteal
from the start of the S ridge of Bruach na Frithe

down a steep corner going left to start then cutting back right before making a couple of steep moves down into the gully.

Traverse of Sgurr na Bairnich (2). Leave the gully at the foot of the abseil and head left (W) up loose scree/path. Veer back right to the ridge and continue to the summit of Sgurr na Bairnich, then descend to the start of Bruach na Frithe's S ridge.

To save time and effort, it's possible to traverse under Sgurr na Bairnich.

❺ S ridge, Bruach na Frithe (2). This involves mainly walking along a rocky ridge with a few short scrambles. The last real difficulty is crossing a small gap, which you enter from the left side of the ridge. Go behind an obvious large rock and traverse a slab rightwards. Continue more easily to the summit of Bruach na Frithe and the only trig point on the ridge.

❻ E ridge, Bruach na Frithe (walk). An easy descent brings you to the foot of the relatively small peak of **Sgurr a' Fionn Choire**. This is easily bypassed to the left (N) but if time and energy allow then it's well worth a detour and provides fantastic views across to the Bhasteir Tooth.

Traverse by W ridge and N face, Sgurr a' Fionn Choire (2/3). Continue on to the W ridge, which has one awkward step, then descend a gully to the N to arrive at Bealach nan Lice.

There are various bivi sites on the start of the spur leading out to Sgurr a' Bhasteir and a spring just below in Fionn Choire with vibrant green moss around it.

Bruach na Frithe to Lice and beyond

Section 10

Bealach nan Lice to Sgurr nan Gillean

Grade	Climbing to Severe and lots of scrambling. Can be reduced to Moderate if Am Basteir is bypassed or approached by the E ridge.
Time	1hr 30min–2hr 30min.
Terrain	Sustained scrambling and climbing, this is very exposed and complex terrain.

Technical climbing and hard scrambling precede the ascent of one of the UK's finest summits. You need to stay switched on and save some energy for the descent and the long slog back to the bar in the Sligachan.

The three options for Am Basteir, in ascending order of difficulty, are: bypass to N, Lota Corrie Route, Naismith's Route.

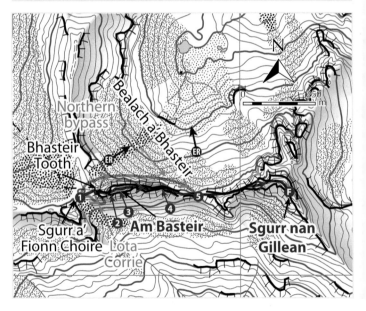

Northern bypass (walk). If things are getting desperate then consider bypassing Am Basteir totally. This is just a walk and may well save the day if energy or daylight are running short.

Descend from Bealach nan Lice and go down scree to the north of Am Basteir. Ascend scree to **Bealach a' Bhasteir** and rejoin the ridge. From here you can continue to Sgurr nan Gillean or tick Am Basteir by its E ridge. The E ridge is mainly easy scrambling but the Bad Step is Difficult to down-climb (it can be abseiled).

1 **Naismith's Route (Severe, 45m), Bhasteir Tooth.** The psychological crux of the ridge, it can seem challenging for the grade, coming as it does at the end of the ridge. It includes outrageous positions on an exposed face.

From Bealach nan Lice, scramble up onto a ridge to the N, which leads to a ledge beneath the obvious overhanging nose of the Bhasteir Tooth. Belays will depend on your rope length and climbing ability of both team members. Several possible belay stances are included which can be used or passed.

Climbers on the Bad Step, Am Basteir

Am Basteir **3**

Naismith's Route, Bhasteir Tooth
(Severe, 45m) and
continuation to
Am Basteir

The Bad Step

4

Bhasteir
Tooth

vii

Bhasteir Nick

vi

2

Lota Corrie Route

iii   iv   v

ii

i

Descent to Lota Corrie Route

i

ⓘ Pitch 1 (10m). Belay using a large block/thread anchor.

Traverse along the ledge onto the S face. There's a possible belay on a ledge with a perfect crack for swallowing a Rock 8 or Rockcentric 3.

ⓘⓘ Pitch 2 (30m). Climb ledges and corners, first up right, then back left and up to a long ledge. The belay at the end of pitch 2 is at **ⓥⓘ**.

ⓘⓘⓘ Traverse the horizontal ledge with scant protection possibilities until the ledge narrows and a light grey scar marks a missing flake. Given the lack of gear and the impending crux move, some will opt to place a Rock 3 high above the start of the ledge and extend it with a 240cm sling.

ⓘⓥ The ledge narrows by a light grey scar where once a flake existed.

You have two choices here. Either climb up boldly using a positive pocket. Then, after a couple of moves, the angle eases and you will reach a wide crack and as many gear placements as you could wish. Or, where the ledge narrows, step awkwardly across to a flake.

ⓥ The flake offers a possible belay.

The flake takes a sling but isn't 100% solid and will certainly end up sometime as another flake scar. It can be backed up by a higher Rock placement.

Climb the flake and then a crack, which curves back left.

The route now swallows gear including threads (120cm slings), and Rockcentric 3 and 4 placements. Follow the crack up to the right with an awkward mantle shelf onto a ledge to finish. A spike behind the ledge provides a bomber belay from where the second can be kept in sight.

ⓥⓘ From the belay, 5m of easy scrambling leads up to the slab top of the Bhasteir Tooth. Follow the slab to the summit of the Tooth.

ⓥⓘⓘ Retrace your route down to the **Bhasteir Nick**, a deep cleft separating the Bhasteir Tooth from Am Basteir.

② **Bhasteir Nick to Am Basteir (Severe).** Leave the Nick, climb a short cleft and traverse right to an enclosed gully, which you should follow for 15m staying immediately right of the dyke. Easy slabs lead to a steep wall and cave blocking progress.

The slabs carry on up and left. Climb steeply up from just left of the cave (4b, 8m) then traverse back right above the cave. The initial few moves require some hard, out-of-balance climbing before you reach the good holds. It's steep and unprotected. A chockstone is turned using the right wall then scramble up to a thread belay, which is often in place where people have abseiled the route going in the opposite direction (as in the winter traverse). Enjoyable scrambling will take you to the summit.

Alternatively, various grooves in the right wall below the small cave avoid the overhang completely and lead to the summit but are more sustained routes.

As another option, carry on up slabs to the left of the cave to an undercut corner known as The Mouth. It's well protected and safe but hard (5b), and can often be overcome with combined tactics.

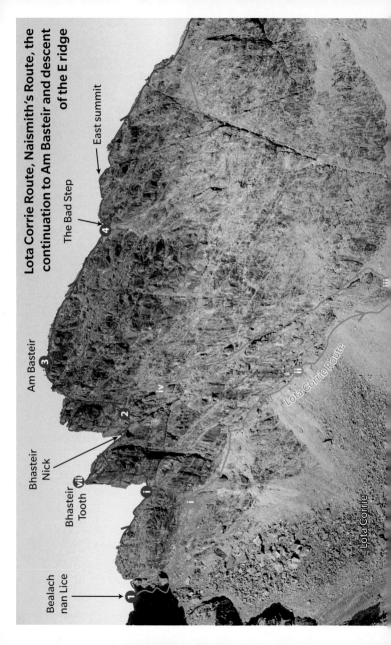

Lota Corrie Route, Naismith's Route, the continuation to Am Basteir and descent of the E ridge

East summit

The Bad Step

Am Basteir

Bhasteir Nick

Bhasteir Tooth

Bealach nan Lice

Lota Corrie Route

Lota Corrie

Lota Corrie Route (Moderate). A classic scramble, this is a much easier and faster alternative than Naismith's Route. The loss of height is the only downside. In many ways, it's more in keeping with the rest of the ridge than the technical climbing of Naismith's Route on the Tooth. It's a classic route and the hardest part is finding it; lots of people don't descend far enough to reach it.

Descend into the top of Lota Corrie. This is further than most people think, but don't be tempted to climb steep rocks too soon or be lured by abseil slings where previous people have made this mistake. Stay tight under the SW face of Am Basteir.

ⓘ Pass below a possible direct start to Naismith's (Difficult).

ⓘⓘ Continue past a distinctive overhang and possible bivi site 50m before the lowest point of the face.

ⓘⓘⓘ Go round the base of the rocks and up scree to an easy angled gully leading back towards the Tooth. Ascend the gully, initially on a cone of scree and then a narrower groove before crossing to the left edge. Pass a big drop down to the left then climb up via small chockstones and avoid a larger chockstone by rocks to the left. The gully can be followed further but it is better to take an exposed slab to the left and back right to rejoin the original line. A high step up and right lets you move onto a boulder in a cleft.

ⓘⓥ Start up the right hand of two grooves before stepping left to the other groove, which is followed to a grassy recess. Step left and climb a slabby rib to easy ground. Traverse left and down a grade 2 slot/chimney to reach the Bhasteir Nick.

❸ **E ridge, Am Basteir (Difficult).** This part is mainly grade 2 and walking, except for a few moves on The Bad Step. Descend easily to The Bad Step.

❹ **The Bad Step** is a short steep wall 3–4m high, which involves a couple of Difficult moves. It's not hard but very exposed with huge drops, so be careful at this late stage of the ridge traverse.

The Bad Step can be bypassed to the right (Lota Corrie) side but although the route is much easier, it's not as obvious as sticking to the ridge.

❺ W ridge, Sgurr nan Gillean (Moderate). Leave the bealach and head E for 200m towards Sgurr nan Gillean. Follow a path/ledge left to bypass the first step of the W ridge. This ledge overlooks Coire a' Bhasteir and ends below a large recess, which has Tooth Chimney at the back left of it. If you plan to descend via the west ridge then packs can be left at the bealach.

ⓘ Tooth groove and arête (Moderate). This is the easiest line to overcome the steep initial part of the ridge. It starts from the ledge approximately 5m before the recess. Climb the groove/chimney above the ledge to reach the narrow crest of the ridge above.

The base of a fallen *gendarme* (pillar) is passed by some airy moves to reach a large block at the top of Tooth Chimney that usually has an abseil sling. If you intend to descend the W ridge, then leave your climbing gear here, and packs as well – depending on conditions.

Tooth Chimney option (Difficult). Classic chimney climbing, which is a useful alternative if things are busy, it joins the arête higher than the exposed moves of the previous route. From the large recess, climb the left-hand chimney. The crux is passing a chockstone.

Once the initial climb is done, 300m of easy scrambling up rocks (grade 2) and scree leads to the summit. Head up towards an obvious pinnacle. Follow the easy terrain to a volcanic pipe of concrete-like rock left of the ridge. Ascend this to the **pinnacle**. Traverse around to the left side of the pinnacle.

ⓘⓘ Go through 'the window' in the pinnacle to access the narrow summit ridge, which is traversed on its right side.

Relax and enjoy the views from this airy summit if time allows. Remember that things aren't finished until you are safely back at the road so remain switched on for the descent.

W ridge, Sgurr nan Gillean (Moderate)

stinctive pinnacle

F

ii

arête

Tooth Chimney ascends the line of the abseil

abseil

Tooth Groove

i

ledge

recess

Bealach a' Bhasteir   5

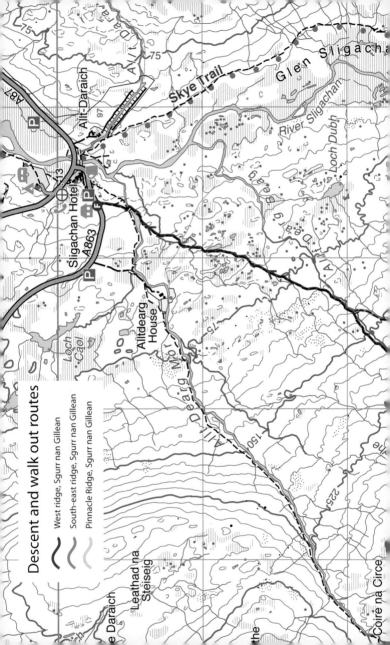

Descent and walk out routes

〰 West ridge, Sgurr nan Gillean
〰 South-east ridge, Sgurr nan Gillean
〰 Pinnacle Ridge, Sgurr nan Gillean

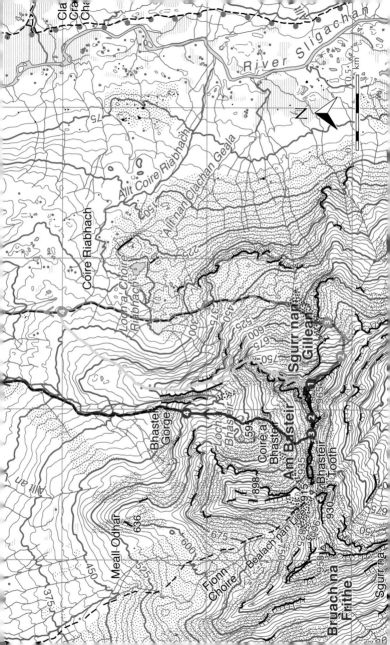

Descent and walk out

Descent 1
West ridge, Sgurr nan Gillean

Grade	Moderate downclimb or grade 2/3 scrambling and an abseil
Time	2–2hr 30min
Terrain	Mainly easy scrambling and an abseil then rough walking before reaching path down in Coire a Bhastier.

This is the quickest descent, which has the advantage of still being fresh in your memory from the ascent. Note: the numbered waypoints below relate to the Descent and walk out map, not the W ridge, Sgurr nan Gillean, topo.

❶ Scramble and walk down to the large block above Tooth Chimney, which usually has an array of abseil slings. The abseil is longer than a 35m rope doubled so take care and knot the rope ends.

❷ A 35m rope will get you past the main difficulties and it's fairly easy to scramble down to the ledge. The abseil can be missed by descending the airy ridge, passing the remains of a missing pillar and down-climbing Easy Chimney (Moderate). Follow the ledge then turn right and descend to Bealach a' Bhastier.

❸ From Bealach a' Bhastier, go down loose screes to the N and descend into **Coire a' Bhastier**. Unless you are familiar with the route, then keep your eyes open for signs of a path and general erosion.

❹ Take care on the descent of slabs to the W of the **Bhasteir Gorge** and be aware of the big drop on your right into the gorge. Once below the gorge, it's an easy walk on a path, which improves as you get closer to the **Sligachan**.

Descent 2
South-east ridge, Sgurr nan Gillean

Grade	3
Time	2–3hr
Terrain	Mainly easy scrambling then rough walking until path is reached in Coire Rhibach.

This is the easiest descent but it can be hard to follow in poor visibility or at night. Do not underestimate this descent. It has the major psychological disadvantage of heading in the opposite direction to the Sligachan, its bar and your celebratory drinks.

1 Leave the summit by the narrow crest, which is level at first, and follow it for about 70m then descend to the right to a wide rake about 50m from the crest. Once this rake has been descended, follow broken ledge systems on the Coire Harta side of the ridge before traversing left under the steep upper section of the ridge. Then descend on the Glen Sligachan side of the ridge to reach a small col with a distinctive square-shaped boulder in it.

2 From the small col, descend scree and boulders to reach the head of a gully.

3 Descend the scree filled gully which is initially quite well defined with steep sides but then widens out lower down. As the terrain levels off, traces of a path lead round towards **Coire Riabhach**. Steep zigzags lead down to level ground and a significantly better path, which leads to a huge cairn.

4 At the cairn, ignore the turning left and carry straight on, cross a single plank footbridge and turn right. Continue on the path to a larger bridge, which is crossed and leads to the main road. Turn right to reach the Sligachan Hotel and Seumas' Bar for a celebratory drink or two.

Descent 3
Pinnacle Ridge, Sgurr nan Gillean

Grade	Difficult
Time	2–3hr
Terrain	Serious scrambling and down climbing before reaching path above Bhastier Gorge.

This is the ultimate way down and the grand finale to the traverse. Prior knowledge will be essential for all but the most experienced teams. At the end of a long day or two days, it's a serious undertaking and only appropriate for the most experienced people who have either done Pinnacle Ridge before, or who have sufficient mountaineering ability to follow their nose. If your team has the energy and mental stamina, then it cannot be too highly recommended.

See Practice Route 8 in the Guidebook for a full description of Pinnacle Ridge.